SharePoint 2013 Solution Series Volumes 11-15

Volume 11

Moving Central Admin to a Different Drive in SharePoint 2013

STEVEN MANN

Moving Central Admin to a Different Drive in SharePoint 2013

Copyright © 2013 by Steven Mann

Trademarks

All terms mentioned in this book that are known to be trademarks or service marks have been appropriately capitalized. The author and publisher cannot attest to the accuracy of this information. Use of a term in this book should not be regarded as affecting the validity of any trademark or service mark.

Screenshots of Microsoft Products and Services

The screenshots of Microsoft Products and/or Services are being "used with permission from Microsoft" based on the copyright guidelines available on Microsoft.com:

http://www.microsoft.com/About/Legal/EN/US/IntellectualProperty/Permissions/Default.aspx

There is no intention of being disparaging, defamatory, or libelous to Microsoft, any of its products, or any other person or entity.

Warning and Disclaimer

Every effort has been made to make this book as complete and as accurate as possible, but no warranty or fitness is implied. The information provided is on an "as is" basis. The author and the publisher shall have neither liability nor responsibility to any person or entity with respect to any loss or damages arising from the information contained in this book.

Introduction

This guide steps through process of moving the Central Administration (Central Admin) web site to a different drive. By default, the Central Administration web site is created on the C: drive using the default inetpub web site location. Many times administrators would like all of the web sites to run on a different drive, such as E:, since C: is a System Drive. While creating Web Applications, you may specify the location; the creation of Central Admin does not give you that option. You can easily move Central Admin to a different drive following the simple steps in this guide.

The same steps are possible in SharePoint 2007 and SharePoint 2010.

Required Steps

Step 1: Navigate to the SharePoint Central Administration and select Manage Web Applications

Application Management
Manage web applications
Create site collections
Manage service applications
Manage content databases

Step 2: Select the Current SharePoint Central Administration web application

Name

SharePoint - 80

SharePoint Central Administration v4

Step 3: Extend the Web Application

From the Web Applications top ribbon menu, click on the Extend button:

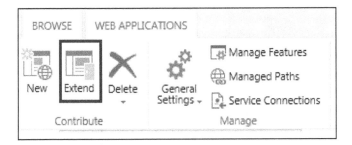

Step 4: Specify the Port and Location

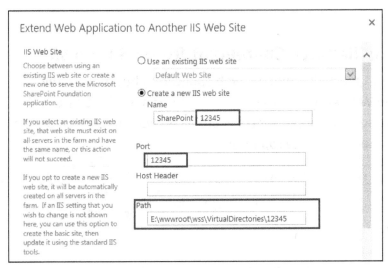

This is where you specify the new non-C-drive location.

Step 5: Verify the URL and the Zone

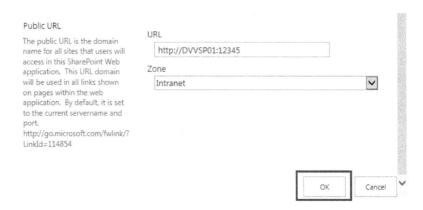

Click OK.

Step 6: Remove SharePoint from IIS Web Site

You aren't really deleting the web application but back on the Manage Web Applications page, with the SharePoint Central Administration web application selected, you need to click on Delete button menu from the top ribbon:

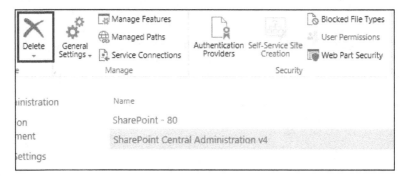

Select Remove SharePoint from IIS Web Site:

Step 7: Select the Original Central Admin Web Site

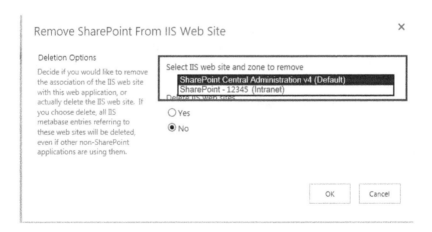

In the Remove SharePoint From IIS Web Site dialog, make sure the original Central Admin web application name is selected. Make sure Delete IIS Web Sites is set to Yes. Click OK.

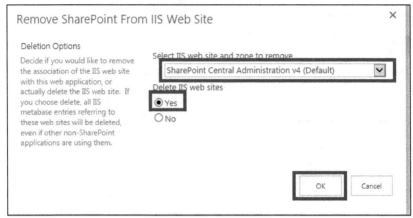

Since you are removing the IIS site (and port) from which you are currently administrating SharePoint, you will receive an error:

This page can't be displayed

- Make sure the web address http://dvvsp01:26897 is correct.
- Look for the page with your search engine.
- Refresh the page in a few minutes.

This means that the old site is down and now Central Admin is running on the new port that you specified during the extending process.

Step 8: Run the SharePoint 2013 Products Configuration Wizard

The SharePoint 2013 Central Administration menu item won't navigate to the new location until the configuration wizard is run.

Conclusion

In less than 10 main steps you can easily move Central Admin to a different drive and insure that there are no web applications running off of the C: system drive. The same steps are possible in SharePoint 2007 and SharePoint 2010 as well.

Volume 12

Installing and Configuring Project Server 2013 in SharePoint 2013

STEVEN MANN

Installing and Configuring Project Server 2013 in SharePoint 2013
Copyright © 2013 by Steven Mann

Trademarks

Screenshots of Microsoft Products and Services

Warning and Disclaimer

Introduction

This guide walks through the installation and initial configuration of Project Server 2013 within a SharePoint 2013 environment.

Creating the Application Server

Project Server 2013 when integrated with SharePoint 2013 runs as a Service Application. Therefore the service should run on one or more Application Servers. Depending on your farm's usage of other services, you may want to scale out your architecture and include dedicated servers for Project Server 2013.

Installing SharePoint 2013 Prerequisites

On the new application server, launch the SharePoint 2013 installation:

Click on the Install software prerequisites link:

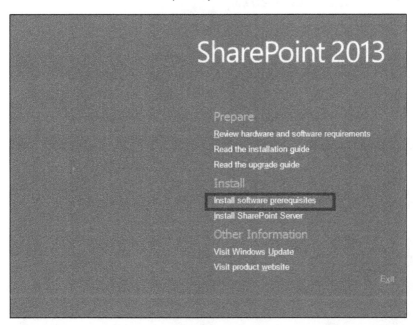

The SharePoint 2013 installation installs and configures the necessary prerequisite software and configures the server roles and features. Several reboots of the server may be necessary.

Installing SharePoint 2013

After the prerequisites have been installed, the next step is to install SharePoint 2013 and join the server to your existing SharePoint 2013 farm.

Return to the SharePoint 2013 Installation (splash) screen and click on Install SharePoint Server:

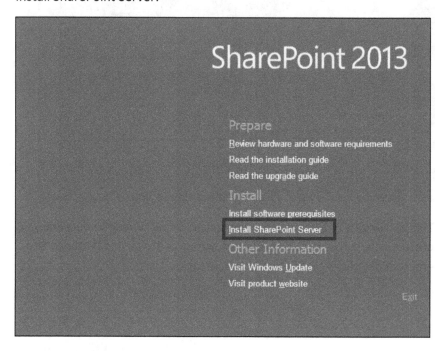

Make sure that the Complete option is selected under Server Type:

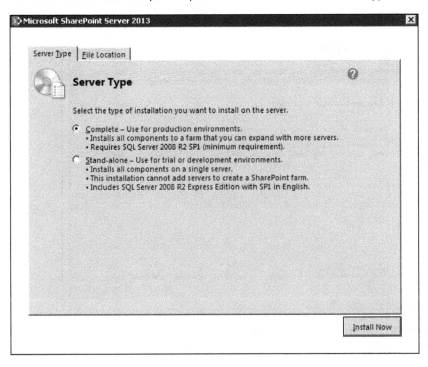

Click on the File Location tab and change the location if necessary:

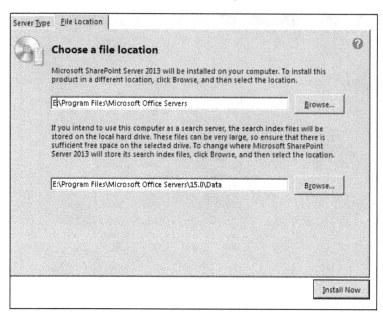

Click on the Install Now button.

SharePoint is installed on the server:

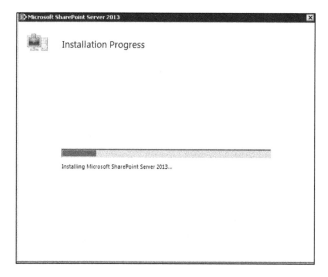

Once the installation is completed, the Run Configuration Wizard dialog appears:

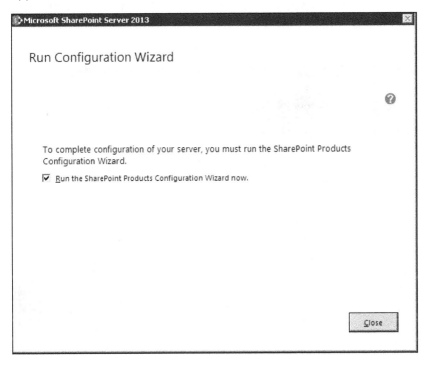

Leave the checkbox checked and click on the Close button.

The SharePoint Products Configuration Wizard runs to join the application server to the existing SharePoint 2013 farm.

Joining the Application Server to the SharePoint Farm

After the installation is complete, the SharePoint Products Configuration Wizard needs to run. Leaving the checkbox checked and clicking Close from the previous process starts the wizard:

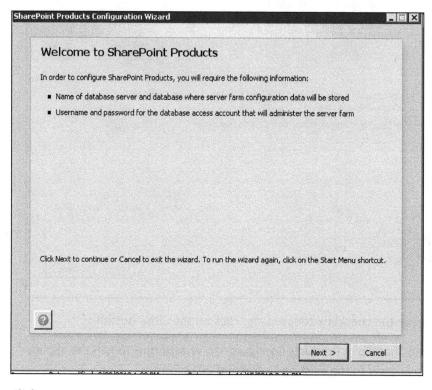

Click Next.

You are warned that services will be "bounced" during the operations:

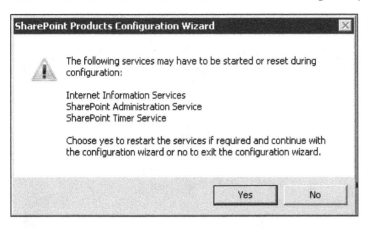

Click Yes.

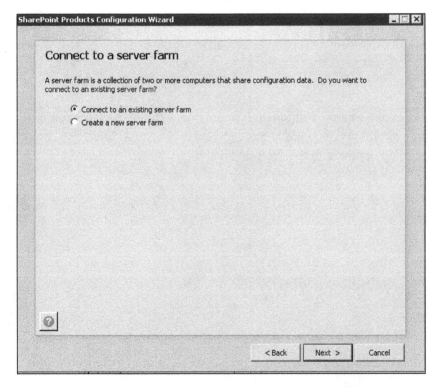

Make sure the Connect to an existing farm is selected and click Next.

The Specify Configuration Database Settings dialog appears. Type in the Database server name in the text box and click the Retrieve Database Names button.

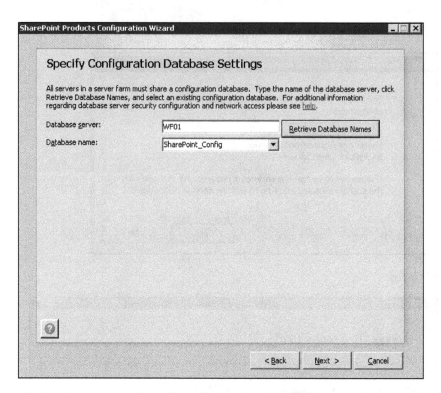

The Database name drop-down is populated with the available configuration databases. Technically there should only be one. Select the configuration database in the drop-down and click Next.

Enter the Farm Passphrase that was used when creating your SharePoint farm initially:

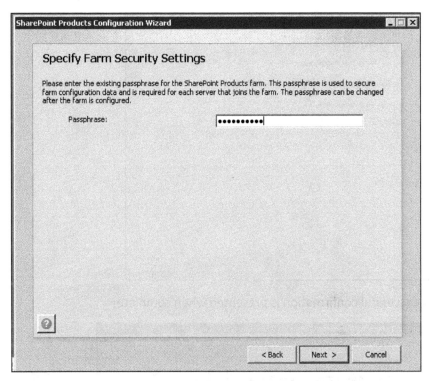

Click Next.

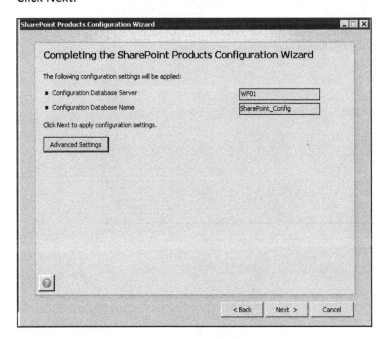

Click Next again. SharePoint is configured and the server is joined to your existing farm:

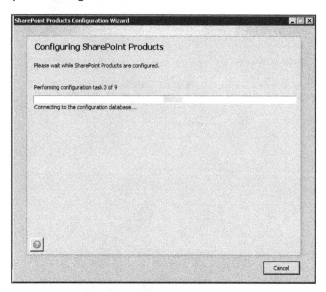

A successful confirmation is presented when complete:

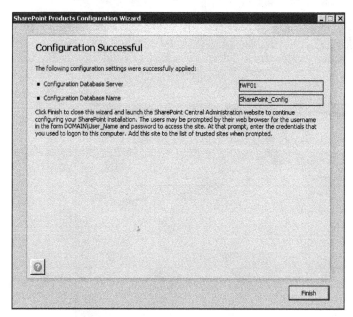

Click Finish.

Installing Project Server 2013

Installing Project Server 2013 on the Application Server

Now that SharePoint is installed on your Application server and the server is joined to the farm, it is time to install Project Server 2013.

Locate the installation media and double-click on the splash.hta file:

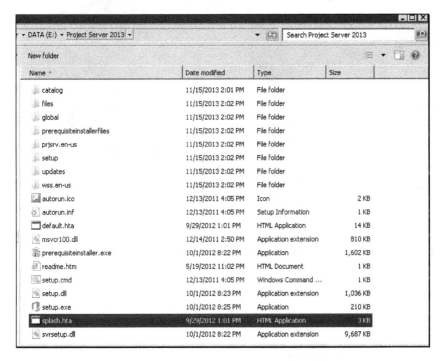

The Project Server 2013 installation splash screen appears:

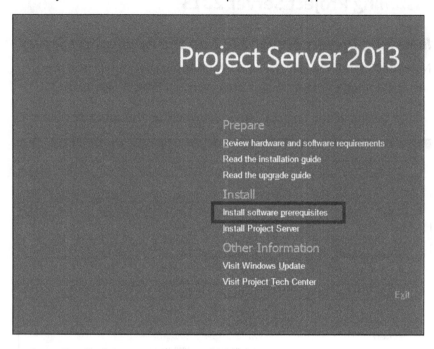

Technically all of the prerequisites should be satisfied but just for good measure you may click on the Install software prerequisites link to verify.

Once the prerequisites have been installed or verified, return to the Project Server 2013 installation splash screen and click on the Install Project Server link:

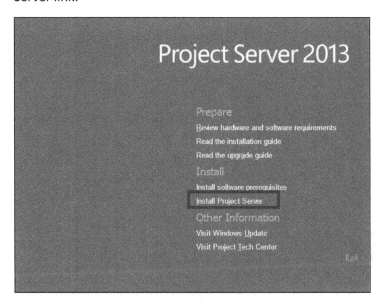

The installation files are prepared:

Enter your Project Server 2013 Product Key when prompted:

Click Continue.

Read the terms of service and check the "I accept" checkbox:

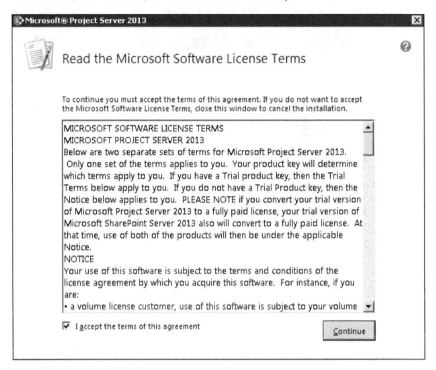

Click Continue.

Since you are installing this on SharePoint, the file location is already determined by where SharePoint was installed:

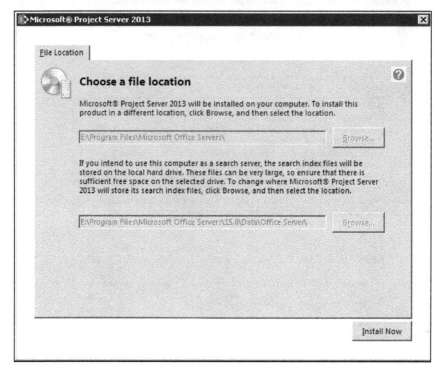

All you need (or can) do here is click Install Now.

Project Server 2013 is installed on the server:

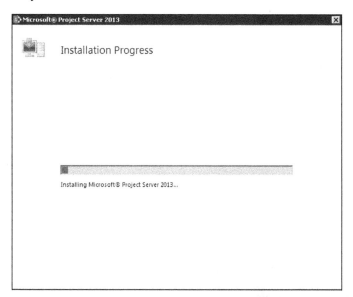

Once installed, it takes a few minutes to finalize:

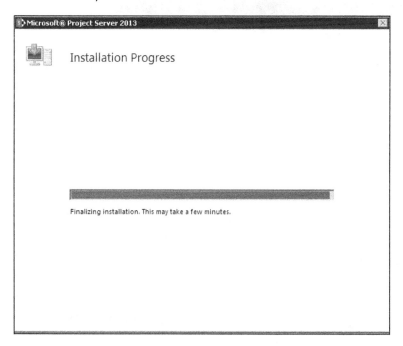

Once completed a similar Configuration Wizard screen appears:

DO NOT RUN THE WIZARD AT THIS TIME!

Uncheck the checkbox and click close:

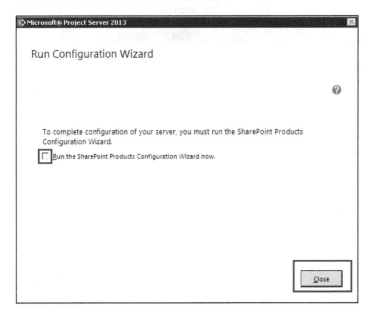

Repeat Project Server Installation on SharePoint Servers

The reason you can't run the configure wizard at this time is because Project Server 2013 now needs to be installed on all of the other servers (except the database server) in your SharePoint farm.

Repeat the steps in the previous section to install Project Server 2013 on each of the other servers.

Running SharePoint Products Configuration Wizard on Each Server

After you have installed Project Server 2013 on each of the servers in your farm, you now must run the SharePoint Products Configuration Wizard on each server separately to upgrade SharePoint. It is always recommended to run the wizard on the server that runs Central Administration first and then continue onto the other servers.

To run the wizard, From the Start menu on each server, under Microsoft SharePoint Products, click on the SharePoint 2013 Products Configuration Wizard.

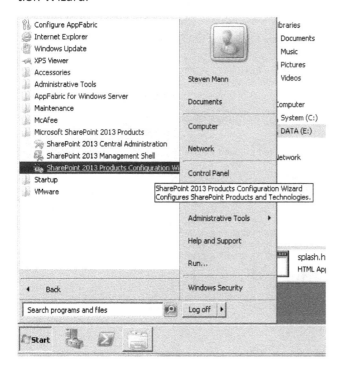

Click Next on the Welcome screen. The warning about bouncing the services appears:

Click Yes.

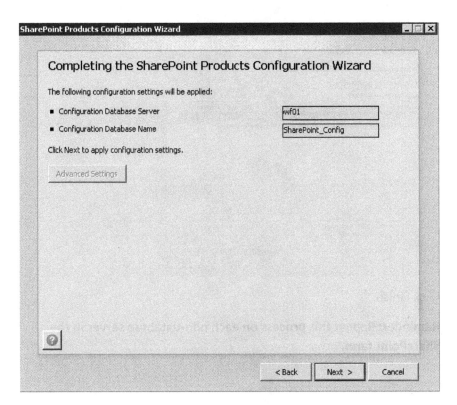

Click Next.

SharePoint is configured.

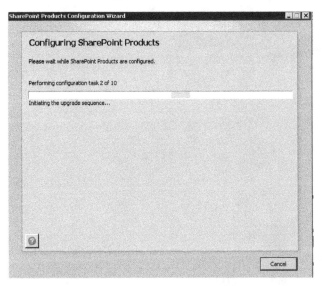

After the configuration is completed, the successful completion screen appears:

Click Finish.

Reminder: Repeat this process on each non-database server in the SharePoint farm.

Provisioning the Service Application and Service

Creating the Project Server 2013 Service Application

Now that Project Server 2013 is installed on the farm, you are able to create the service application. You do this in Central Administration.

In Central Administration, click on the Manage Service Applications link under Application Management.

On the Manage Service Applications page, from the New drop-down menu select Project Server Service Application.

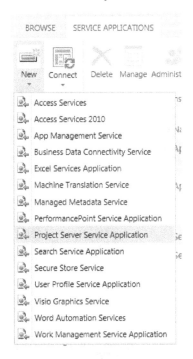

The Create Project Services Application dialog appears:

Enter a name for the service application and either select an existing application pool or select the option to create a new application pool and provide a name for the new pool. I personally try to use the same app pool when possible. This reduces the amount of worker processes that run and reduces memory consumption.

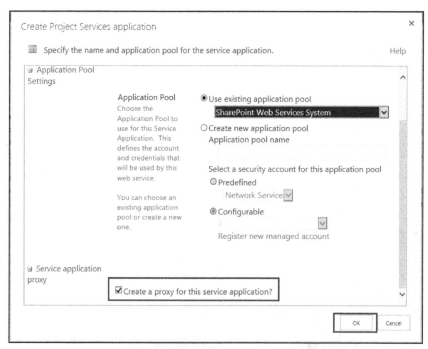

At the bottom of the dialog, make sure the proxy checkbox is checked and click OK.

The Project Server Service Application is created and now appears in the list of service applications.

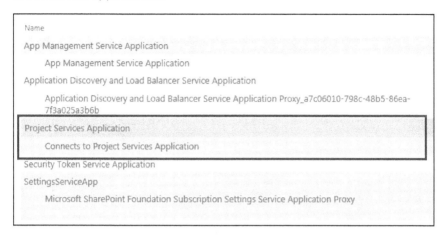

Select the new service application and then click on the Administrators button from the Service Applications top ribbon:

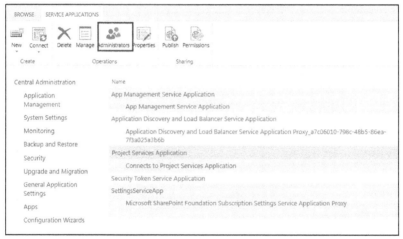

Enter the accounts in the first box and click Add:

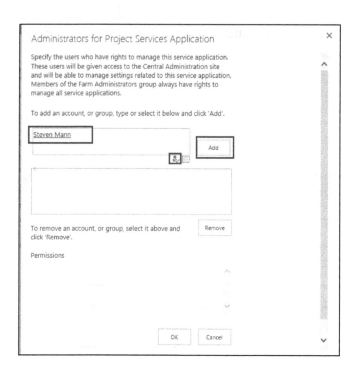

I at least add myself and the main service account.

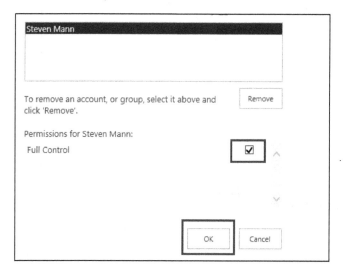

Select each account in the list and check the Full Control check box. Click OK when complete.

With the service application still selected, click on the Permissions button from the top ribbon:

Administrators Properties   Publish Permissions

)perations   Sharing

Name

App Management Service Application

    App Management Service Application

Application Discovery and Load Balancer Service Application

    Application Discovery and Load Balancer Service Application Proxy_a7c06010-798c-48t
7f3a025a3b6b

Project Services Application

    Connects to Project Services Application

Security Token Service Application

SettingsServiceApp

    Microsoft SharePoint Foundation Subscription Settings Service Application Proxy

Add the groups or accounts that should access the Project Server 2013 functionality. I usually just add Everyone if this will be used by the general user population:

Connection Permissions for Project Services Application

Specify the accounts or other principals that have access to invoke this service application.

To add a claim, type or select it below and click 'Add'.

Everyone

Add

Local Farm
Steven Mann

To remove a claim, select it above and click 'Remove'.   Remove

Permissions for Local Farm:

Full Control   ☑

OK   Cancel

Once again, select each Account in the list and make sure the Full Control checkbox is checked.

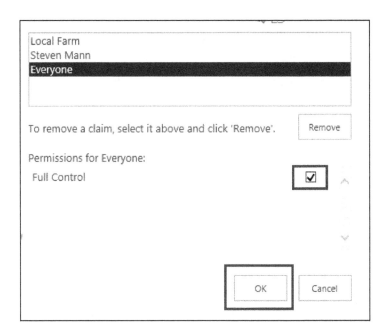

Click OK.

Starting the Project Server 2013 Services

Before you can manage the service application, the service needs to be running on at least one server. Therefore, from the left-hand navigation, select Application Management.

Central Administration	Name
Application Management	App Management Service Application
	App Management Service Application
System Settings	Application Discovery and Load Balancer Service
Monitoring	Application Discovery and Load Balancer Se
Backup and Restore	7f3a025a3b6b
Security	Project Services Application
	Connects to Project Services Application
Upgrade and Migration	Security Token Service Application
General Application Settings	SettingsServiceApp
Apps	Microsoft SharePoint Foundation Subscript
Configuration Wizards	

Under the Service Applications section, click on the Manage services on server link:

Service Applications
Manage service applications   Configure service application associations   Manage services on server

Databases
Manage content databases   Specify the default database server   Configure the data retrieval service

Select each server from the top where the service should run. Locate the Project Server Application Service in the list of services and click Start.

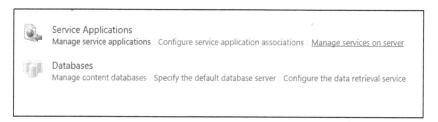

PerformancePoint Service	Stopped	Start
PowerPoint Conversion Service	Stopped	Start
Project Server Application Service	Stopped	Start
Request Management	Stopped	Start
Search Host Controller Service	Stopped	Start

Refresh the page until the service is Started:

Microsoft SharePoint Foundation Workflow Timer Service	Started	Stop
PerformancePoint Service	Stopped	Start
PowerPoint Conversion Service	Stopped	Start
Project Server Application Service	Started	Stop
Request Management	Stopped	Start
Search Host Controller Service	Stopped	Start

Creating and Configuring the Project Web App

Creating the Project Web App Instance

Now that the service(s) are running, return to the Manage Service Applications page, select the Project Server Service Application, and click on the Manage button from the top ribbon:

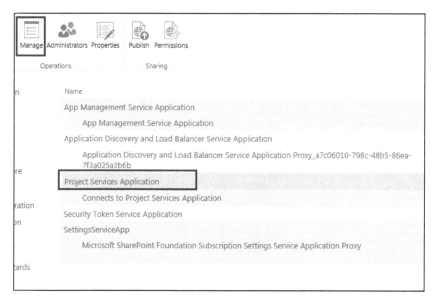

The Manage Project Web Apps page appears. Click on the Create Project Web App Instance:

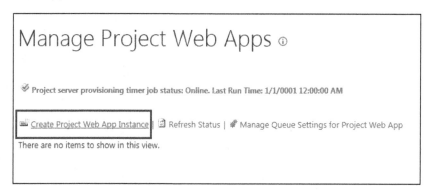

The Create Project Web App Instance page appears. Select the Web Application that you want to use for the Project Web App and enter the Project Web App path (or use the default PWA).

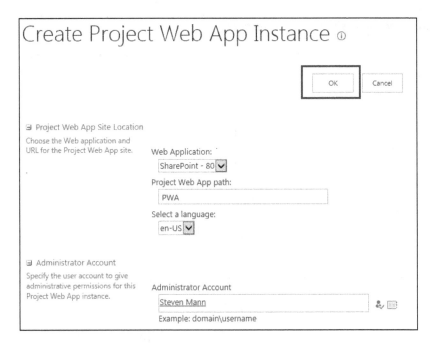

The Project Web App path becomes an explicit managed path under the root of the web application. So if you select the SharePoint - 80 web application and your server/dns name is sp2013, the Project Web App Instance will be created under http://sp2013/PWA.

Enter an Administrator account and click OK on the Create Project Web App Instance screen after making your selections.

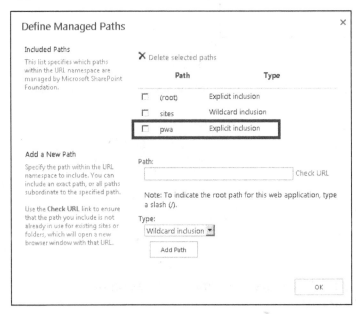

Screen above is shown as a reference.

The Project Web App instance is created and cycles through various statuses:

Status
Waiting for Resources.

Creating Project Web App Site.

Status
Configuring the new Project Web App Site.

Status
Provisioning Database.

The Project Web App instance is complete when the status changes to Provisioned:

Status
Provisioned

Navigate to your PWA site to verify the creation. (e.g. http://sp2013/PWA)

Configuring PWA to Allow Local Base Calendars

While you are verifying the PWA site, it is a good time to modify a calendar setting such that schedule dates are preserved and not changed when publishing a project to SharePoint.

From your PWA site, select PWA Settings from the Settings menu (gear):

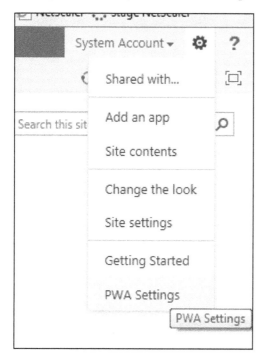

On the PWA Settings screen, under Operational Policies, click on the Additional Server Settings link:

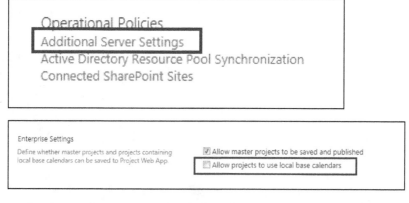

Under Enterprise Settings, check the Allow projects to use local base calendars checkbox.

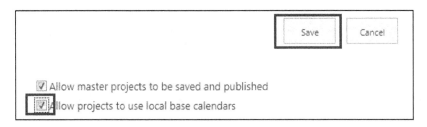

Click Save.

Using Microsoft Project 2013 with the Project Web App

Connecting Microsoft Project 2013 to the Project Web App

Now each user must connect their local Microsoft Project 2013 application to the SharePoint-based Project Web App.

First launch Microsoft Project 2013 on a local machine:

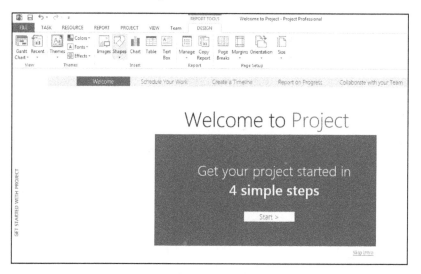

Click on the FILE menu at the top left.

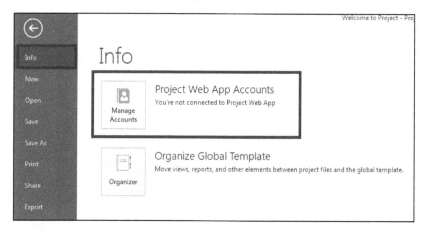

On the Info screen notice under Project Web App Accounts that you are not connected to the Project Web App. Click on the Manage Accounts button.

The Project Web App Accounts dialog appears:

Click on the Add... button.

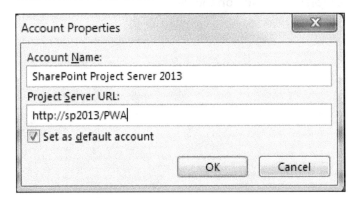

Enter a name for the account and the URL to your Project Web App site. Check the Set as default account checkbox and click OK.

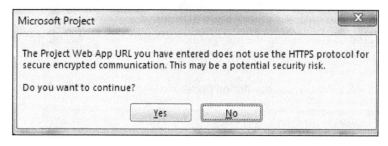

If you are warned about not using HTTPS, click Yes on the message. The new account is added to the list of Project Web App accounts.

Make sure the new account is set as the default and click OK.

Now you must close and re-open Microsoft Project 2013 in order to connect the Project Web App in SharePoint.

Upon re-opening Microsoft Project 2013, you will see that you are now connected to the Project Web App on the Info page:

Info

Software Development Plan

My Documents

Permissions

Decide who can do what with your project.

Project Web App Accounts

SharePoint Project Server 2013

Connected as i:0#.w|steven mann

Organize Global Template

Move views, reports, and other elements between project files and the global template.

Publishing a Project File to SharePoint

Once a local project file is ready for publishing, from Microsoft Project 2013, click on FILE and then Info:

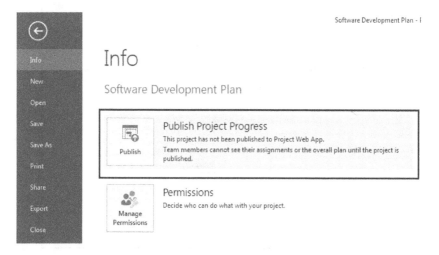

Click on the Publish button.

If you receive a message about the Enterprise Standard Calendar, refer to the Configuring PWA to Allow Local Base Calendars section of this guide before proceeding.

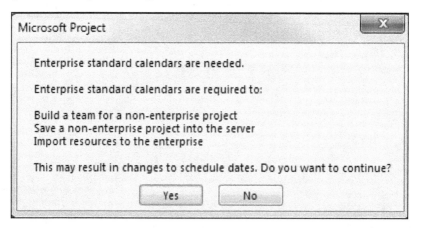

On the Publish Project dialog, enter a site URL and click Publish:

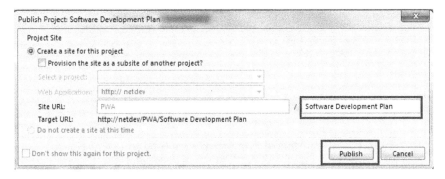

To keep the URLs clean of spaces, you may want to remove any spaces in the URL and then change the Title of the site that is created.

The project is published to SharePoint and a new site is created under the Project Web App path:

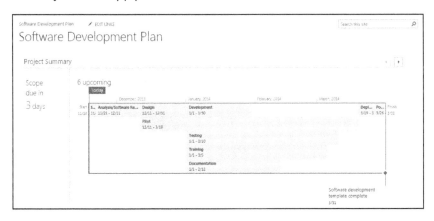

Conclusion

It is very easy to install and configure Project Server 2013 within SharePoint 2013. I hope you found this information useful and easy to use. If there are any questions or problems, please send them to steve@stevethemanmann.com

Volume 13

Optimizing SharePoint 2013: Application Pools

STEVEN MANN

Optimizing SharePoint 2013: Application Pools

Copyright © 2013 by Steven Mann

Trademarks

Screenshots of Microsoft Products and Services

Warning and Disclaimer

Introduction

SharePoint 2013 is very robust and powerful. All of this robustness and power comes with a price: resources. If you have twenty available servers and can scale-out like crazy, you shouldn't have any problems. However, most of us don't have that many servers at our disposal; especially for QA and development environments.

Therefore, it is important to tweak and configure SharePoint 2013 such that you get the performance and functionality without utilizing too many resources.

This guide explores various areas and options for both Web and Service Application Application Pools such that minimal resource usage is achieved in both Development/QA environments as well as Production.

Check out the other optimization areas in Steve's solution series or get them all together in _Optimizing Your SharePoint 2013 Environments_.

WEB APPLICATION APP POOLS

Web Application App Pool Overview

When you specify a new app pool for web applications in Share-Point, an application pool is created in IIS. Each application pool results in an IIS Worker Process:

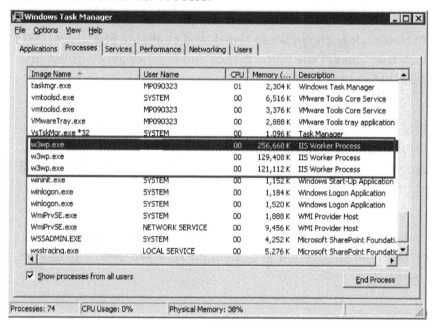

Each worker process takes up memory and CPU resources. Therefore, the more worker processes, the more resources are being used. Sharing application pools may be advantageous to reducing overall memory consumption.

Initial Web Applications

Before you create any web applications, the installation of Share-Point creates the Central Administration web application and site. Along with this is an IIS (App Pool) although SharePoint stores information about this app pool as well. This app pool should be dedicated to Central Admin

When you create other web applications, you get to choose whether to create a new app pool or use an existing one. Creating the main SharePoint web application produces an IIS Web Site on Port 80 by default and creates a SharePoint - 80 application pool accordingly.

Creating Additional Web Applications

Since most application pools are storing similar information and take up lots of memory, you may easily share app pools between web applications to reduce the consumption of resources.

DEV/QA

When creating a new SharePoint Web Application, instead of creating a new application pool, select an existing one:

Production

You may do the same thing in Production only if you know the additional web applications will not be very large. If multiple web applications are very large in size, the application pool may take on too much memory and then decide to automatically recycle. This can be an ongoing occurrence if the shared app pool is always large.

Combining Existing App Pools

If you already have your environment built out, you may combine web applications such that they use the same app pool. Doing this via IIS does not allow SharePoint to control it and any new web front ends will not follow suit. Therefore, you need to use PowerShell to implement this correctly.

DEV/QA

In Development or QA environments, there are usually only a few people hitting the SharePoint sites and Central Admin. Therefore, if resources are low, you may easily modify your web applications such that they all use the same app pool. There is no harm in development and QA environments.

In my development environment, I wanted to modify Central Admin to use the same app pool as my main SharePoint web application (on port 80). Therefore, I would be combining the two separate app pools into one:

Application Pools

This page lets you view and manage the list of application pools on the server. Application pools are associated with worker proce

Filter: ▼ 🔍 Go   ▼ 🔍 Show All | Group by: No Grouping   ▼

Name ▲	Status	.NET Frame...	Managed Pipeli...	Applications
007deca21913445aa767537ad5c130b7	Started	v4.0	Integrated	1
ASP.NET v4.0	Started	v4.0	Integrated	0
ASP.NET v4.0 Classic	Started	v4.0	Classic	0
Classic .NET AppPool	Started	v4.0	Classic	0
DefaultAppPool	Started	v4.0	Integrated	1
faf081e07ff74f54be65d0123c85c3c0	Started	v4.0	Integrated	2
SecurityTokenServiceApplicationPool	Started	v4.0	Integrated	3
SharePoint - 80	Started	v4.0	Integrated	1
SharePoint Central Administration v4	Started	v4.0	Integrated	1
SharePoint Web Services Root	Stopped	v4.0	Integrated	1

The previous state is that I have two separate application pools, one for the Central Admin web application and one for the main SharePoint web application.

Opening up SharePoint 2013 Management Shell, I can apply these commands to perform the modification:

Get the source web application (main SharePoint web application on port 80)

$sourceWebApp = Get-SPWebApplication http://sp2013:80

Get the target web application (Central Admin)

$targetWebApp = Get-SPWebApplication http://sp2013:50555

Set the target application pool to the source application pool

$targetWebApp.ApplicationPool = $sourceWebApp.ApplicationPool

Provision and Update

$targetWebApp.ProvisionGlobally()

$targetWebApp.Update()

Reset IIS

Iisreset

After performing this operation, I now only have one application pool for both Central Admin and my main SharePoint web application:

 Application Pools

This page lets you view and manage the list of application pools on the server. Application pools are associated with worker proce

Name ▲	Status	.NET Frame...	Managed Pipeli...	Applications
007deca21913445aa767537ad5c130b7	Started	v4.0	Integrated	1
ASP.NET v4.0	Started	v4.0	Integrated	0
ASP.NET v4.0 Classic	Started	v4.0	Classic	0
Classic .NET AppPool	Started	v4.0	Classic	0
DefaultAppPool	Started	v4.0	Integrated	1
faf081e07ff74f54be65d0123c85c3c0	Started	v4.0	Integrated	2
SecurityTokenServiceApplicationPool	Started	v4.0	Integrated	3
SharePoint - 80	Started	v4.0	Integrated	2
SharePoint Central Administration v4	Started	v4.0	Integrated	0
SharePoint Web Services Root	Stopped	v4.0	Integrated	1

So now SharePoint - 80 is servicing 2 applications and the Central Admin App Pool is now servicing 0 applications. You may remove the Central Admin app pool from IIS now. SharePoint will still know about the app pool if you ever wanted to set Central Admin back. See http://stevemannspath.blogspot.com/2013/06/sharepoint-2013-listing-out-existing.html for more details.

I also have one less IIS Worker Process running and taking up memory on my development machine.

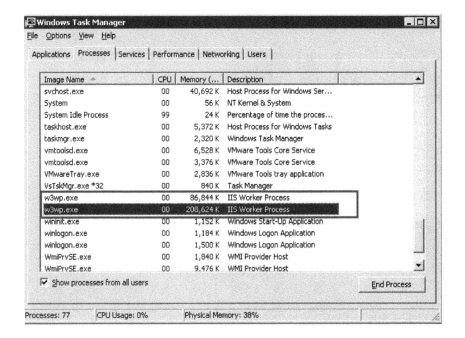

You may use the same PowerShell commands to combine other web applications so instead of using the Central Admin URL you would insert the other web application URL as the target.

Production

In Production, I would keep Central Admin and the main Share-Point web application running in separate app pools. You don't need something to go wrong and you can't get to Central Admin to fix (for example).

You could combine other web application pools but as I stated in the previous section, this all depends on the expected size of the web applications.

If anything, try to limit the amount of web applications and try to just use one web application for your SharePoint sites. This means using SharePoint - 80 to host My Sites as well.

SERVICE APPLICATION APP POOLS

Service Application App Pool Overview

When you specify a new app pool for service applications in SharePoint, an application pool is created in IIS. Each application pool results in an IIS Worker Process:

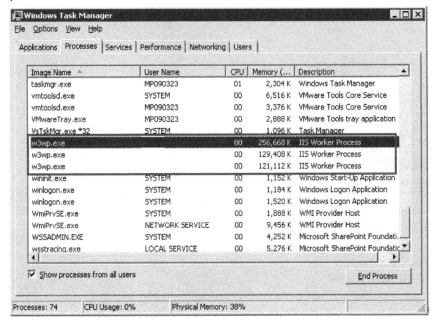

Each worker process takes up memory and CPU resources. Therefore, the more worker processes, the more resources are being used. Sharing application pools may be advantageous to reducing overall memory consumption.

Initial Creation of Service Applications

When you create service applications from the UI or from PowerShell, you can specify whether to use an existing application pool or to create a new one.

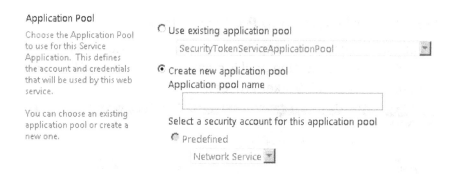

The default selection is to create a new one.

DEV/QA

For any development environment or QA environment, select the Use existing application pool option and select the out-of-the-box SharePoint application pool, "SharePoint Web Services System":

Production

Production is slightly different. While most service applications can run using the SharePoint Web Services System application pool, there are certain service applications that are recommended to use their own application pool.

The Secure Store Service is one of these, for example, because of security purposes. The Security Token Service (STS) already gets created using a separate app pool and changing this via Central Admin is not an option as the properties are disabled (and PowerShell doesn't allow it either). I would leave STS alone in Production.

Changing the Service Application App Pools

You may change the service application app pools via PowerShell or via the Central Admin UI.

PowerShell

If you going to use PowerShell to update the service application pools, you first need to know the identities (guids) of the service applications.

Run Get-SPServiceApplication in the SharePoint 2013 Management Console to list out the current service applications and their guids:

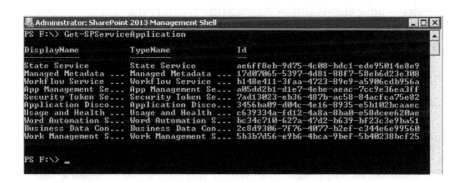

Now use those Ids for the source and targets in the following commands.

```
# Get the Source Service Application

$sourceServiceApp = Get-SPServiceApplication -Identity 17d07065-5397-4d81-88f7-
58eb6d23e308


# Get the Target Service Application

$targetServiceApp = Get-SPServiceApplication -Identity 2c8d9306-7f76-4077-b2ef-
c344e6e99560


# Set the Target Service Application App Pool

$targetServiceApp.ApplicationPool = $sourceServiceApp.ApplicationPool


# Update the Target Service Application

$targetServiceApp.Update()
```

Central Admin UI

This is one case where I find it easier just to change something using the UI versus PowerShell. In Central Admin, click on Manage Service Applications under Application Management:

For each service application in which you may have created a separate app pool, select it from the list and click on the Properties button from the top ribbon:

If the Properties button is disabled, then you automatically know that the app pool cannot be changed and it should be left alone.

Change the Application Pool to use the built-in SharePoint Web Services System application pool and click OK:

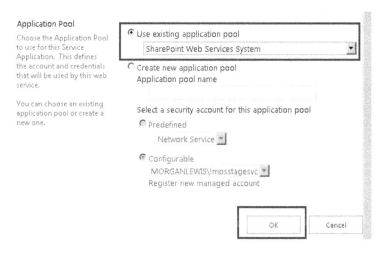

Repeat for each service application.

DEV/QA vs. Production

In development and QA environments, I would combine as many app pools as possible and have all available service applications share the SharePoint Web Services System application pool.

I already mentioned that certain service application should run within their own application pool (Secure Store Service). Therefore in Production I would create only separate app pools for these cases. Otherwise I would use the SharePoint Web Services System app pool for all others to share.

Conclusion

This is just one of several areas that you may tweak to improve performance and reduce resource utilization. Check out the other optimization areas in Steve's solution series or get them all together in _Optimizing Your SharePoint 2013 Environments_.

I hope you found this guide useful and informative. If you have any troubles or other questions, please send them to me at steve@stevethemanmann.com.

Volume 14

Optimizing SharePoint 2013: Logging

STEVEN MANN

Optimizing SharePoint 2013: Logging

Copyright © 2013 by Steven Mann

Trademarks

Screenshots of Microsoft Products and Services

Warning and Disclaimer

Introduction

SharePoint 2013 is very robust and powerful. All of this robustness and power comes with a price: resources. If you have twenty available servers and can scale-out like crazy, you shouldn't have any problems. However, most of us don't have that many servers at our disposal; especially for QA and development environments.

Therefore, it is important to tweak and configure SharePoint 2013 such that you get the performance and functionality without utilizing too many resources.

This guide explores various SharePoint logging options such that minimal resource usage is achieved in both Development/QA environments as well as Production. The areas covered are as follows:

- Health Analyzer
- Diagnostic Logging
- Usage and Health Data Collection
- IIS Web Logs

Check out the other optimization areas in Steve's solution series or get them all together in _Optimizing Your SharePoint 2013 Environments_.

HEALTH ANALYZER

SharePoint Health Analyzer Overview

The SharePoint Health Analyzer warns on various conditions that may require attention on your SharePoint farm. Many times you'll see the warning when loading Central Admin:

⊗ The SharePoint Health Analyzer has detected some critical issues that require your attention.

There are several pages of health condition rules that may or may not be applicable in all environments. Therefore, why have Share-Point do more work when it is not necessary?

DEV/QA

In development and QA environments, these health warnings will probably go ignored and only sometimes will they be resolved by the developer or QA manager. It is not production and most of the time people don't worry about these warnings.

▲Category : **Security** (2)

    The server farm account should not be used for other services.

    Accounts used by application pools or service identities are in the local machine Administrators group.

▲Category : **Performance** (2)

    Databases exist on servers running SharePoint Foundation.

    The paging file size should exceed the amount of physical RAM in the system.

▲Category : **Configuration** (4)

    Databases require upgrade or not supported.

    Missing server side dependencies.

    Outbound e-mail has not been configured.

    Databases running in compatibility range, upgrade recommended.

▲Category : **Availability** (2)

    Drives are running out of free space.

    Drives are at risk of running out of free space.

Rules tend to be broken in development and QA because they are not full-fledged production environments.

Therefore, if you have the time, I would go into the conditions and disable most of the rules in development and QA.

Select Monitoring from the Central Admin left navigation:

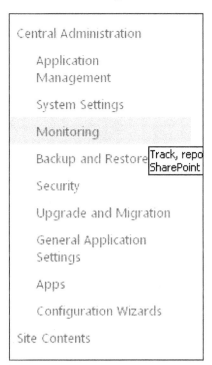

Click on the Review rule definitions link:

Click on each rule definition link you wish to disable:

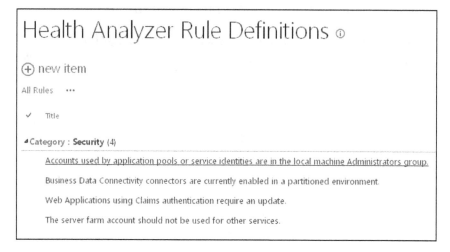

Click on the Edit Item button on the top ribbon:

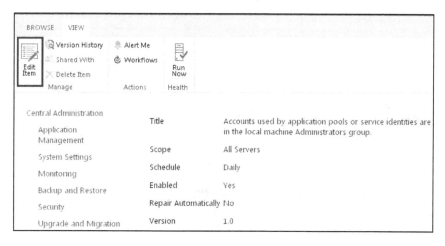

Uncheck the Enabled checkbox and click Save:

Title *	Accounts used by application pools or service identities are in the l
Scope *	All Servers ▼
	The rule scope determines where the rule file is run. If the rule scope is set to All, the rule file will run on all computers with the specified service. If the rule scope is set to Any, the rule file will run on the first available computer with the specified service.
Schedule *	Daily ▼
	Determines when the rules are checked automatically
Enabled *	☑
	If selected, SharePoint will periodically look for this problem.
Repair Automatically *	☐
	If Repair Automatically is selected, SharePoint will attempt to repair errors as soon as they are found.
Version	1.0
	Version
	Save Cancel

Repeat for each additional rule definition.

As an alternative, in development and QA environments, you may turn off the health analyzer all together by disabling all of the timer jobs. See the Timer Jobs and Services guide for more info.

Production

As I stated previously, the health warnings are most likely ignored in development and QA environments, but what about production? In production I don't want to ignore these issues but at the same time I don't want to be warned on some things that I don't need to worry about. Plus I don't need SharePoint doing more work to notify me of something that I may never change.

Before you disable anything in production, wait a week to see what kind of health warnings you receive. Review the issues and determine if they will ever be corrected or if that's just the way it is (such as some of the account rules).

Next disable the rules which fall into this case. For me, I first disabled two account rules. The reason is because some of our service accounts are used for application pools and farm accounts and may have admin privileges. It is not the recommended service account structure but it is what it is and I don't need to be notified that this is an issue; nor do I need SharePoint wasting resources trying to identify this issue and reporting it to me.

Next I disabled the Drives are at *risk* of running out of free space. Why? There is already a rule that warns of drives actually running out of disk space. I don't need to be warned about the risk. This alert was occurring against the C: drive of our servers however there is plenty of free space and since we keep our logs on the E: drive, there shouldn't be any worry. The threshold here deals with the amount of memory on the server and having enough room for logs and memory dump files. I think we are safe; you need to determine your own disk space conditions.

Finally, I changed the Database has large amounts of unused space to run Daily. I want this to be resolved on a daily basis and not have to wait for a week to realize some shrinking needs to occur (or have the amount of unused space grow even larger). I also modified this definition to repair automatically. This will shrink the database as needed.

DIAGNOSTIC LOGGING

Diagnostic Logging Overview

SharePoint uses the Unified Logging System (ULS) to produce logs of various events and actions that are executed, errors that have occurred, critical issues, etc. The logs come in handy when attempting to diagnose problems, however, most of the time they are a waste of resources and disk space.

You may configure the diagnostic logging settings by selecting Monitoring from the Central Admin left navigation:

Central Administration

    Application Management

    System Settings

    Monitoring

    Backup and Restore Track, repo SharePoint

    Security

    Upgrade and Migration

    General Application Settings

    Apps

    Configuration Wizards

Site Contents

Under the Reporting section, click on the Configure diagnostic logging link:

The Diagnostic Logging configuration page is rendered:

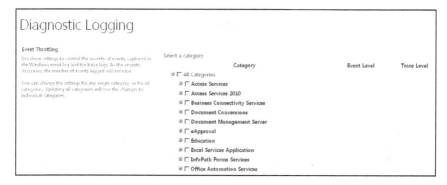

DEV/QA

In development and QA environments, select All Categories and select the least critical events to None:

You don't need SharePoint to log anything unless you are debugging an issue. I would throttle this as needed, keeping your resources available for development and QA testing.

If you have a separate drive other than C: in development and QA, change the path to the log file to use the other drive. This prevents writes to the system drive. Also, change the number of days to store log files down to a low number such as 1 or 2. This will take up less disk space and keep your drives a bit cleaner. In development and QA you usually are looking for something when it happens, not several days ago. You don't need to worry about stale log files so why keep them around?

Click OK when completed to save your changes.

Production

In Production, I usually just want to worry about the worse cases unless I am trying to trace something. Therefore, on my production farm, I tend to select All Categories and then set the least critical event log item to Critical and the least critical trace log to Unexpected:

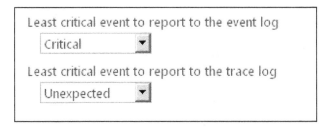

Currently, as of this writing, changing these settings may produce a ton of "Forced due to logging gap" log entries. There doesn't seem to be a workaround or fix for this as of yet but I have seen people complaining on various forums and blogs. The only way I can stop this from happening is to set everything back to the default:

So hopefully this is corrected in a cumulative update (CU) or Service Pack.

Hopefully in Production you have an E: drive (or another drive other than C:) and can change the path of the logs to use that drive. This prevents or limits the writing to the system drive. Also, I tweak the number of days to store the log files to a lower number. In production you don't want it too low (just in case) so I changed mine to 5 days:

Path

E:\Program Files\Microsoft Office Servers\LOGS\

Example: %CommonProgramFiles%\Microsoft Shared\Web Server Extensions\15\LOGS

Number of days to store log files

5

Click OK when completed to save your changes.

USAGE AND HEALTH DATA COLLECTION

Usage and Health Data Collection Overview

In addition to diagnostic logging, SharePoint may log events about the usage of the farm and its components/processes. While this may be helpful in analyzing usage, it is very resource and database intensive. Therefore, usage should be throttled accordingly.

DEV/QA

Unless you need to analyze something, a development SharePoint environment and any staging/QA environment should not really be doing any usage data collection:

☐ Enable usage data collection

Uncheck the option to save unnecessary resource abuse in your non-production environments. Same goes for Events to log. I have them all unchecked on my development server.

Events to log:

- ☐ Analytics Usage
- ☐ App Monitoring
- ☐ App Statistics.
- ☐ Bandwidth Monitoring
- ☐ Content Export Usage
- ☐ Content Import Usage
- ☐ Definition of usage fields for Education telemetry
- ☐ Definition of usage fields for service calls
- ☐ Definition of usage fields for SPDistributedCache calls
- ☐ Definition of usage fields for workflow telemetry
- ☐ Feature Use
- ☐ File IO
- ☐ Page Requests
- ☐ REST and Client API Action Usage
- ☐ REST and Client API Request Usage
- ☐ Sandbox Request Resource Measures
- ☐ Sandbox Requests
- ☐ SQL Exceptions Usage
- ☐ SQL IO Usage
- ☐ SQL Latency Usage
- ☐ Task Use
- ☐ Tenant Logging
- ☐ Timer Jobs
- ☐ User Profile ActiveDirectory Import Usage

You may also uncheck the Enable health data collection option as well:

☐ Enable health data collection

Click the link below to edit the health logging schedule.
  Health Logging Schedule

Production

Production is a bit different. You may want to track usage of your SharePoint farm. If this is the case, enable usage data collection:

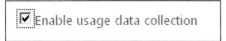

☑ Enable usage data collection

However, only log the events that you truly care about tracking:

Events to log:
   ☐ Analytics Usage
   ☐ App Monitoring
   ☑ App Statistics.
   ☐ Bandwidth Monitoring
   ☐ Content Export Usage
   ☐ Content Import Usage
   ☐ Definition of usage fields for Education telemetry
   ☐ Definition of usage fields for service calls
   ☐ Definition of usage fields for SPDistributedCache calls
   ☐ Definition of usage fields for workflow telemetry
   ☑ Feature Use
   ☐ File IO
   ☑ Page Requests
   ☐ REST and Client API Action Usage

Again, it is also a good idea to keep the logs on a separate drive to reduce the writes on the C: system drive:

Log file location:

E:\UsageLogs

Health data collection is good to run in production so you may be forewarned of any issues:

☑ Enable health data collection

Click the link below to edit the health logging schedule.
Health Logging Schedule

Clicking on the Health Logging Schedule allows you to tweak the timer job frequencies. For the most part they run Daily or Hourly and seem to be pretty well behaved. I would leave these alone and worry about disabling the jobs that aren't necessary (see the Timer Jobs and Services Guide in the Solutions Series).

IIS WEB LOGS

Web Logs Overview

SharePoint web applications run under IIS, so of course, regardless of SharePoint, IIS itself produces logs of any web access.

Logging in IIS is configured at each web site. Selecting a web site, such as the SharePoint - 80 web application and then clicking Logging in the main window opens the Logging dialog.

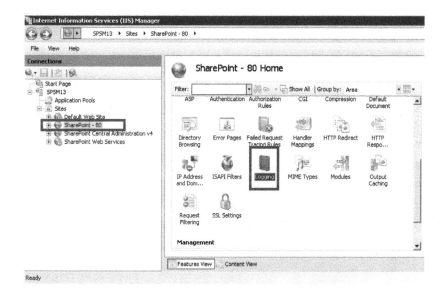

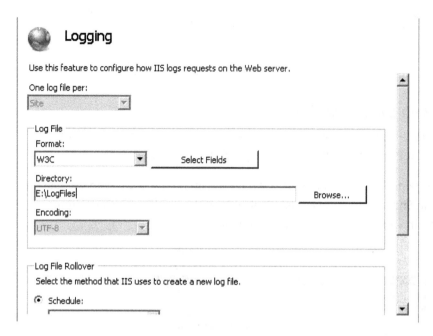

No matter what environment, switching the location of the log files to a drive other than C:, reduces disk writes to the system drive.

DEV/QA

In development and QA/Staging environments, there really is no reason to have IIS pounding away at the log files. You already have SharePoint doing its fair share of using disk resources. Therefore, there is no harm in disabling the IIS logging for all web applications on these servers.

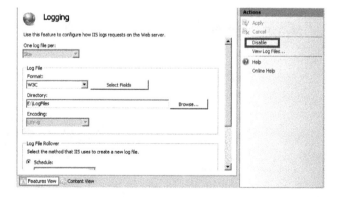

Production

If you are not using the IIS logs for access analysis and tracking in production, I would disable the IIS logging for each web application in IIS.

Conclusion

These are just some of several areas that you may tweak to improve performance and reduce resource utilization. Check out the other optimization areas in Steve's solution series or get them all together in *Optimizing Your SharePoint 2013 Environments*.

I hope you found this guide useful and informative. If you have any troubles or other questions, please send them to me at steve@stevethemanmann.com.

Volume 15

Optimizing SharePoint 2013: Timer Jobs and Services

STEVEN MANN

Optimizing SharePoint 2013: Timer Jobs and Services

Copyright © 2013 by Steven Mann

Trademarks

Screenshots of Microsoft Products and Services

Warning and Disclaimer

Introduction

SharePoint 2013 is very robust and powerful. All of this robustness and power comes with a price: resources. If you have twenty available servers and can scale-out like crazy, you shouldn't have any problems. However, most of us don't have that many servers at our disposal; especially for QA and development environments.

Therefore, it is important to tweak and configure SharePoint 2013 such that you get the performance and functionality without utilizing too many resources.

This guide explores various areas and options for Timer Jobs and Services such that minimal resource usage is achieved in both Development/QA environments as well as Production.

Check out the other optimization areas in Steve's solution series or get them all together in _Optimizing Your SharePoint 2013 Environments_.

TIMER JOBS

Timer Jobs Overview

Timer jobs are scheduled processes that perform various functions to keep SharePoint running smoothly. These jobs are run by the SharePoint Timer Service which is constantly running on the SharePoint farm servers:

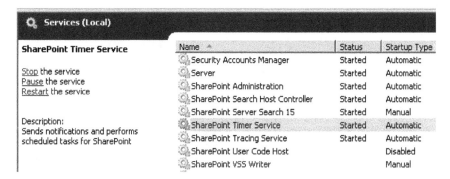

The service program is OWSTIMER.EXE:

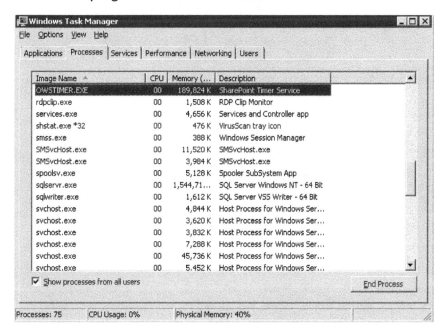

It is constantly running and does take up some memory, however, you can reduce the amount of work it needs to perform by tweaking the timer jobs that need to run.

To do this, first select Monitoring from the Central Admin left navigation:

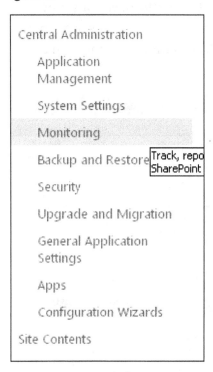

Under the Timer Jobs section, click on the Review job definitions link:

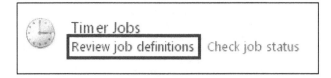

On the Job Definitions page, select each timer job definition you want to disable:

Job Definitions

Title

Analytics Event Store Retention

App Installation Service

App State Update

Application Addresses Refresh Job

Application Server Administration Service Timer Job

Application Server Timer Job

Audit Log Trimming

Autohosted app instance counter

Bulk workflow task processing

CEIP Data Collection

Cell Storage Data Cleanup Timer Job

Change Log

Content Organizer Processing

Content Type Hub

On the Edit Timer Job page, click the Disable button to disable the timer job:

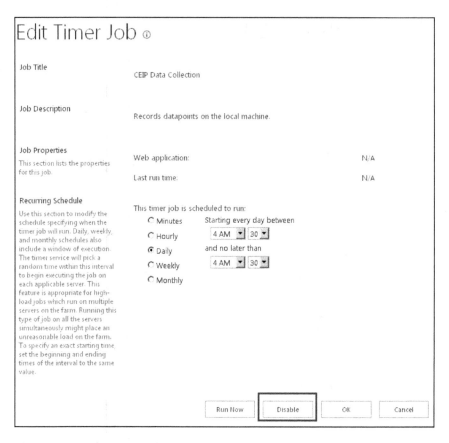

Edit Timer Job ⓘ

Job Title

CEIP Data Collection

Job Description

Records datapoints on the local machine.

Job Properties

This section lists the properties for this job.

Web application: N/A

Last run time: N/A

Recurring Schedule

Use this section to modify the schedule specifying when the timer job will run. Daily, weekly, and monthly schedules also include a window of execution. The timer service will pick a random time within this interval to begin executing the job on each applicable server. This feature is appropriate for high-load jobs which run on multiple servers on the farm. Running this type of job on all the servers simultaneously might place an unreasonable load on the farm. To specify an exact starting time, set the beginning and ending times of the interval to the same value.

This timer job is scheduled to run:

- ○ Minutes
- ○ Hourly
- ● Daily
- ○ Weekly
- ○ Monthly

Starting every day between

4 AM ▼ 30 ▼

and no later than

4 AM ▼ 30 ▼

Run Now   Disable   Ok   Cancel

The Timer Job is now disabled:

Audit Log Trimming	SharePoint - 80	Monthly
Autohosted app instance counter		Weekly
Bulk workflow task processing	SharePoint - 80	Daily
CEIP Data Collection		Disabled
Cell Storage Data Cleanup Timer Job	SharePoint - 80	Daily
Change Log	SharePoint - 80	Weekly

Timer Jobs to Disable

The Timer Jobs that you should disable deal with the services or features that you are not using in any environment. Therefore the ones to choose in development, QA, and production all depend on the answer to the question, "Am I using this feature?"

Some jobs may already be disabled based on your tweaking of the Diagnostic Logging, Health Collection, and Usage settings. So besides those, here are the timer jobs that stand out as questionable:

CEIP Data Collection: Are you participating in the Customer Experience Information Program? No? Disable

eDiscovery In-Place Processing: Are you using the eDiscovery services in SharePoint? No? Disable

Education Bulk Operation: Education Services was never officially released! Disable

Holds Processing and Reporting: Are you using holds anywhere?

SharePoint Server CEIP Data Collection: Are you again participating in the Customer Experience Information Program?

Variations jobs (multiple): Are you using variations anywhere in SharePoint?

Most jobs that need to run, execute in seconds if not milliseconds. So disabling these only makes a small difference in memory and performance. The overall feeling here is that the less SharePoint has to do, the better it can perform the things it needs to do.

SERVICES ON SERVER

This section of the guide is designed mainly to bring your attention to services that may be running on Production servers that do not need to be running. In a Development or QA/Staging environment, where servers are limited (if not singular), you may not be able to stop or remove these services.

Services on Server Overview

The Services on Server may be accessed via Central Admin by clicking the Manage services on server link under System Settings:

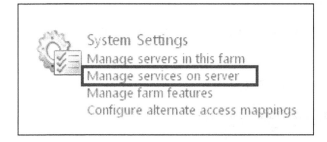

This brings up the Services on Server page:

Services on Server ⓘ

Server: spsm13 ▾ | View: Configurable ▾

Service	Status	Action
Access Database Service 2010	Stopped	Start
Access Services	Stopped	Start
App Management Service	Started	Stop
Business Data Connectivity Service	Stopped	Start
Central Administration	Started	Stop
Claims to Windows Token Service	Stopped	Start
Distributed Cache	Started	Stop
Document Conversions Launcher Service	Stopped	Start
Document Conversions Load Balancer Service	Stopped	Start
Excel Calculation Services	Stopped	Start
Lotus Notes Connector	Stopped	Start
Machine Translation Service	Stopped	Start

This page displays all of the main SharePoint services (which mostly correlate to Service Applications but not all) that may be stopped or started on the selected server.

By using the Server drop-down, you may navigate to each server in the current farm by changing the server:

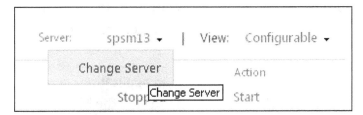

For best reference on which services should run on each server, check out the Plan Service Deployment article on TechNet (http://technet.microsoft.com/en-us/library/jj219591.aspx)

The key takeaway here is to make sure that you aren't bogging down your servers with services that shouldn't be running on them.

Microsoft SharePoint Foundation Web Application

When you install SharePoint on any server, the installation assumes that it is going to be a web front end. Therefore the IIS web sites and all of the web application goodness (services) are installed and processes are fired up and started.

So this means that even when you are configuring an application server, the web sites are copied over and installed. This means that application pools are running and IIS Worker Processes are taking up memory and CPU.

Therefore, after installing and configuring an application server (including dedicated Search servers), you can stop the Microsoft SharePoint Web Application service:

Microsoft SharePoint Foundation Sandboxed Code Service	Stopped	Start
Microsoft SharePoint Foundation Subscription Settings Service	Stopped	Start
Microsoft SharePoint Foundation Web Application	Started	Stop
Microsoft SharePoint Foundation Workflow Timer Service	Started	Stop
PerformancePoint Service	Stopped	Start
PowerPoint Conversion Service	Stopped	Start

Since this is configured to run on all web servers, many people forget that it doesn't need to run on the non-web-front-end servers.

Microsoft SharePoint Foundation Workflow Timer Service

The SharePoint Foundation Workflow Timer Service is also configured to run on all web servers so it is installed and fired up after installation. Again, this service does not need to run on the application servers - so it can be stopped on any non-web-front-end server as well:

Microsoft SharePoint Foundation Incoming E-Mail	Stopped	Start
Microsoft SharePoint Foundation Sandboxed Code Service	Stopped	Start
Microsoft SharePoint Foundation Subscription Settings Service	Stopped	Start
Microsoft SharePoint Foundation Web Application	Started	Stop
Microsoft SharePoint Foundation Workflow Timer Service	Started	Stop
PerformancePoint Service	Stopped	Start

Claims to Windows Token Service

The Claims to Windows Token Service (C2WTS) only needs to run on servers that run the Excel Services service and/or PerformancePoint Services. The TechNet documentation also states that it needs to run on any server running a service application that needs to pass SharePoint identities to external data sources.

While additional configuration is required for SQL Server 2012 and accessing external data, the C2WTS doesn't need to run on all of your servers in the farm.

Distributed Cache

By default the Distributed Cache is installed and started on every installation. Not only does the Distributed Cache service not need to run on every server, you will get warned if it is running on too many servers in the farm. In fact, with this "bad-boy", not only should it be stopped but also removed from the servers that it does not need to run.

Essentially this service should run only on the web front end servers unless you have a Distributed Cache and Request management tier. Then it should only run on the servers participating in the Distributed Cache and Request management tier and not the web front end servers.

To remove this service from the servers that do not need them, you need to run the following PowerShell commands on each server separately:

```
Stop-SPDistributedCacheServiceInstance -Graceful
Remove-SPDistributedCacheServiceInstance
```

Conclusion

This is just one of several areas that you may tweak to improve performance and reduce resource utilization. Check out the other optimization areas in Steve's solution series or get them all together in *Optimizing Your SharePoint 2013 Environments*.

I hope you found this guide useful and informative. If you have any troubles or other questions, please send them to me at steve@stevethemanmann.com.